P9-ELG-295

CH

DISCARD
MAY 2014
Westminster Public Library
3705 W. 112th Ave.
Westminster, CO 80031
www.westminsterlibrary.org

PLANET ARK

Preserving Earth's Biodiversity

Written by
Adrienne Mason

Illustrated by
Margot Thompson

CitizenKid™

A collection of books that inform children about the
world and inspire them to be better global citizens

Kids Can Press

For Alexander. A beautiful world awaits — A. M.

For Neddy — M. T.

Acknowledgments

Thank you to the following people for their assistance: Hussein Alidina, Marine Science and Planning, World Wildlife Fund Canada; Dr. Barbara Beasley, Association of Wetland Stewards for Barkley and Clayoquot Sounds; Dr. Susanna Fuller, Marine Conservation Coordinator, Ecology Action Centre, Halifax, NS; Bob Hansen, Department of Wildlife, Government of Nunavut; Dr. Maja Krzic, Faculty of Forestry/Faculty of Land and Food Systems, University of British Columbia; Prof. Wim van der Putten, Department of Terrestrial Ecology, Netherlands Institute of Ecology.

CitizenKid™ is a trademark of Kids Can Press Ltd.

Text © 2013 Adrienne Mason
Illustrations © 2013 Margot Thompson

All rights reserved. No part of this publication may be reproduced, stored in a retrieval system or transmitted, in any form or by any means, without the prior written permission of Kids Can Press Ltd. or, in case of photocopying or other reprographic copying, a license from The Canadian Copyright Licensing Agency (Access Copyright). For an Access Copyright license, visit www.accesscopyright.ca or call toll free to 1-800-893-5777.

Kids Can Press acknowledges the financial support of the Government of Ontario, through the Ontario Media Development Corporation's Ontario Book Initiative; the Ontario Arts Council; the Canada Council for the Arts; and the Government of Canada, through the CBF, for our publishing activity.

Published in Canada by
Kids Can Press Ltd.
25 Dockside Drive
Toronto, ON M5A 0B5

Published in the U.S. by
Kids Can Press Ltd.
2250 Military Road
Tonawanda, NY 14150

www.kidscanpress.com

The artwork in this book was rendered in acrylic on canvas.
The text is set in Cantoria MT Std.

Edited by Valerie Wyatt
Designed by Marie Bartholomew

This book is smyth sewn casebound. Manufactured in Shenzhen, China, in 10/2012 through Asia Pacific Offset.

FSC
www.fsc.org
MIX
Paper from responsible sources
FSC® C012521

CM 13 0 9 8 7 6 5 4 3 2 1

Library and Archives Canada Cataloguing in Publication

Mason, Adrienne

Planet ark : preserving Earth's biodiversity / written by Adrienne Mason ; illustrated by Margot Thompson.

(CitizenKid)
Includes index.
ISBN 978-1-55453-753-2

1. Ecology — Juvenile literature. 2. Biodiversity — Juvenile literature. 3. Biodiversity conservation — Juvenile literature. 4. Nature — Effect of human beings on — Juvenile literature.

I. Thompson, Margot, 1965– II. Title III. Series: CitizenKid.

QH541.14.M375 2013   j577   C2012-904628-0

Kids Can Press is a Corus™ Entertainment company

Contents

Planet Ark

In the story of Noah's Ark, a flood threatens life on Earth. Noah and his family build a large wooden ark and load the world's animals two by two, with one male and one female of each species. The ark has everything the animals need to survive, including food and fresh water. And they do survive. When the floodwaters subside, Noah and his furry, feathery flock leave the ark and spread out across the land.

In many ways, our beautiful blue home — planet Earth — is like an ark sailing through the universe. It has almost seven billion human passengers and millions of other species, from algae and apes to zucchinis and zebras. And traveling through space with us on our great planetary ark is everything we living things need to survive — food, water and a place to call home.

Planet Ark is rich with life. Scientists have recently estimated that there are about 8.7 million species on Earth, but only a small fraction — about 10 percent — have been identified so far. An amazing 7.6 million species have yet to be discovered. Biodiversity is a word used to describe this amazing abundance of life on Earth. *Bio* means life, and *diversity* means variety. Imagine — as you read this, somewhere on Earth a chorus of frog croaks fills the air, a humming-bird sips sweet nectar from a flower, and a sunflower turns its yellow head to follow the sun. In ditches and deserts, forests and fields, greenhouses and even inside your gut, our world teems with life.

Earth's biodiversity is something to celebrate. It is also a precious heritage that needs our protection, because today, Planet Ark is sailing in troubled waters. Biodiversity is under threat as species become extinct. Although living things have always disappeared over time, the *rate* of extinction has sped up. In the last few centuries, the effects of human actions such as overharvesting, pollution, habitat destruction and more mean that species are being lost faster than ever before.

Thankfully, there are many modern-day Noahs — groups and individuals — who are working hard to preserve Earth's biodiversity. You'll meet some of them in this book and see what they are doing to help protect Planet Ark. And on page 30 you'll find ideas on how you, too, can become a Noah and do your part to care for Earth's biodiversity. Get ready for an exciting voyage. Planet Ark is about to set sail.

Earth is the only known planet with a biosphere, a zone that has all the conditions that make life possible.

Extinct means that a species no longer exists anywhere on Earth. *Endangered* means that the population of a species has become so small that it is at high risk of becoming extinct.

Some scientists calculate that the rate of extinction today is 1000 times faster than during most of Earth's history. A big reason for this is the loss of habitats. For example, in just the last century, about 40 percent of the world's forests have been cut down.

Countries of the world agree that biodiversity is important. As of 2012, 168 countries have signed the Convention on Biological Diversity, a plan to protect Earth's biodiversity.

Biodiversity Times Three

Tropical forests buzz with squawks, whistles and howls. Backyard gardens burst with carrots and corn. Tropical reefs shimmer with rainbow-colored brain corals and butterfly fish. This rich variety of species makes our planet hum and spark with life.

A species is a group of organisms that can breed with one another and produce offspring. Humans are one species (*Homo sapiens*), and pineapples (*Ananas comosus*) are another. Species diversity is one kind of biodiversity — it is the number of different species. For instance, there are about 20 000 species of ants in the world, including leaf-cutter ants, bright orange citronella ants and the ants that steal crumbs at your picnic. But there are two other types of diversity that are also important to life on Earth — genetic and habitat diversity.

You and your friends are both members of the same species, but you are not identical. This is because your genes, with their coded traits, are unique. Genes are the building blocks of a species. Genetic diversity measures the diversity within a species. Planet Ark's genetic diversity is vast, like an ocean of information. But when a species becomes extinct, its genes also disappear.

A rich genetic diversity acts like an insurance plan that protects against extinction. The more genetic diversity within a species, the better chance it can withstand drastic changes, such as drought or disease.

Habitat diversity describes the variety of natural places where organisms live. Earth is covered in a crazy quilt of habitats large and small. The Sahara Desert is a habitat, but so is a drop of water or a muck-filled ditch. Habitats include the living and nonliving things that species interact with, including other plants and animals, the climate, soil, water and much more.

Having a variety of habitats offers a wide range of options for life on Earth. One species might make its home in a steamy, hot jungle, while another survives on the windswept Arctic tundra. When habitats are lost, the species that depend on them may be lost, too.

Biodiversity — of species, genes and habitats — means a richer and more varied planet, but, more importantly, it also means a healthier one. In fact, biodiversity is such an important idea that the United Nations declared 2011 to 2020 as the United Nations Decade on Biodiversity.

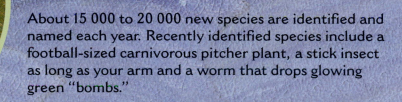

About 15 000 to 20 000 new species are identified and named each year. Recently identified species include a football-sized carnivorous pitcher plant, a stick insect as long as your arm and a worm that drops glowing green "bombs."

Many species share some of the same genes. This pufferfish has about 31 000 genes. Humans have between 20 000 and 25 000 genes. The two species share 961 identical genes. And humans have 7000 genes in common with one kind of tiny nematode worm.

Some places are biodiversity hot spots. Tropical rainforests cover only 7 percent of our planet's land surface but provide habitat for more than half of all species on Earth, including the scarlet macaw.

We humans are all the same species, but humans have many differences, from the foods we eat to the clothes we wear and the homes we live in. The way people live is also shaped by the natural world.

Living and Breathing Biodiversity

Do you love chocolate? Then thank the midges that make chocolate possible. These tiny flies spread pollen from one cacao flower to the next. This fertilizes the flowers so they can produce cacao beans, which are used to make chocolate. Midges are just one kind of pollinator in the world. Bees, other insects and even larger animals, such as bats and birds, also do this important work. And thank goodness they do. One out of every three bites of food you take was made possible by the work of pollinators.

Pollination is one of the many services that biodiversity provides in an ecosystem. (An ecosystem is all of the living things in an environment, as well as the nonliving things — such as climate — that affect them.) "Ecosystem services" result in clean water, rich soil, pure food, breathable air and other qualities that make for a healthy planet. For example, green plants provide the oxygen that animals need to survive. Bacteria and fungi decompose (break down) animals and plants, recycling the nutrients in them to create rich, healthy soil. Birds and other animals spread seeds and control pests. Wetlands and mangroves buffer the impact of high waves on coastlines. The list of ecosystem services is long.

Reduce biodiversity and you also reduce these services, sometimes with disastrous results. Haiti, for instance, has lost 97 percent of its forest in less than 100 years. Hurricanes destroyed some of the forest, but the rest was cut down. Without the forests, soil is eroding, leaving little soil for new plants and polluting the water. This affects not only the trees but also the animals that require forest habitats. Forest loss also affects people. It's hard to grow food when the soil is poor. Fewer species of wild plants and animals mean fewer options for harvesting and hunting in the forest. Today, Haiti is one of the poorest countries in the world. While there are many reasons for the poverty, the destruction of Haiti's forests played an important role.

Earth's living things provide ecosystem services that keep Planet Ark running smoothly. And their work — from cleaning water to creating oxygen — often goes unrecognized until they're gone.

This tiny midge (shown many times its actual size here) is responsible for most of the world's supply of chocolate. It pollinates the cacao blossom, which produces cacao beans, the source of chocolate.

Three-quarters of the world's people depend on medicines that come from plants. Plant extinctions reduce the medicines — those known and those yet to be discovered — available from nature's pharmacy.

The Amazon rainforest is sometimes called the lungs of our planet because it produces over 20 percent of the world's oxygen. Providing oxygen is just one of the forest's many essential ecosystem services.

Every year, pollinators fertilize over a billion dollars' worth of apples, pears, cucumbers, melons, berries and other crops in Canada alone.

The Real World Wide Web

Suppose you were fixing your bike or mounting new wheels on your skateboard and found you had an extra bolt or screw left over when the job was done. Don't toss the "leftovers" away — you might regret it next time you're cruising down a hill. Sometimes things that seem to have no use can turn out to be important. This is one reason people are concerned about the loss of biodiversity. It is impossible to know what we are "throwing away" when we lose

species and damage habitats. Perhaps a spaghetti-thin worm squirming through the soil might help digest a toxic pollutant, or a rare flower in the tropical forest could produce a valuable medicine. When we lose biodiversity, we also lose possibilities.

The world of living things is like a giant interconnected web. The organisms interact with one another in many ways. One of the most common ways is through their stomachs. All animals have to eat, and they are linked

Some rare orchids, like this lady slipper, can only be pollinated by one type of insect. The extinction of the insect would result in the loss of the orchid.

Taxol is an anti-cancer drug found in the bark of the Pacific yew tree. For years, this tree was discarded as a "scrub tree" that had no value to people.

through food chains. In food chains, plants are eaten by herbivores, which are in turn eaten by carnivores. For instance, rabbits eat grass, and lynx eat rabbits. But most animals eat more than one thing — a lynx will also eat mice and birds. So all these food chains intertwine into complex food webs.

Sometimes the interconnections between organisms and their habitats are hard to predict. In Kenyan coral reefs, for example, the overfishing of triggerfish led to a population explosion of their main prey, sea urchins. The urchins then grazed on the pink algae that help coral reefs grow and stay healthy. The loss of the algae damaged the reefs, a critical habitat to many species. This chain reaction helped scientists understand some of the complicated interactions between all of the species living on coral reefs. They also learned the critical role that small, often overlooked organisms such as algae can play.

The pink algae that bind a coral reef together or a screw that holds your pedal to the metal — even the smallest thing has a role to play. Lose even one small "part" of the natural world and we may be in danger of losing something big.

When the sea urchin's main predator became scarce, the sea urchin population exploded. The spiky sea urchins fed on the pink algae that kept coral reefs healthy. Before long, the reefs and many species that depended on them were at risk.

Sometimes it is Earth's smallest things that support the largest. Plankton and tiny shrimplike organisms called krill provide enough nutrition to support the world's largest animal, the blue whale.

The koala bear would be at risk if anything happened to its habitat. So would many other animals that have very specific food or habitat needs.

Today, there are more than 120 000 protected areas in the world. Added together, they would cover an area more than twice the size of Canada.

Marine protected areas help preserve ocean habitats. Fishing is usually not permitted within these areas. This means that there are more fish that can reproduce, which boosts fish populations.

Protected areas help people, too. They deliver ecosystem services such as cleaning water. And protected areas provide jobs. In the African country of Namibia, areas that preserve the habitats of elephants and oryx provide jobs for more than 200 000 people.

The world's largest national park is Northeast Greenland National Park. It has fewer than forty human residents but is home to huge herds of musk oxen, as well as polar bears, walruses, narwhals, hooded seals, Arctic foxes and dozens more mammal and bird species.

Saving Wild Places

What do you need to survive? Every living thing needs a habitat — a place where it has adequate food, water and space to live.

Habitats vary from species to species. Some species inhabit a wide variety of habitats. Coyotes, for example, range throughout most of North America. They live in cities, fields and forests and eat a varied diet that includes small mammals, insects, fruit, birds' eggs and snakes. In contrast, koalas have a very narrow habitat. They live only along Australia's eastern coast, and most of their diet consists of one thing — eucalyptus leaves.

Animals that live in a variety of habitats can adapt to changes more easily than those that have specific needs. If a coyote loses one food source, it can move on to another. But if a koala doesn't have access to eucalyptus trees, it is not likely to survive.

Many kinds of animals migrate, or move, between two or more habitats throughout the year. Amphibians, including frogs and salamanders, often breed in one location and then feed in another. Birds, whales, butterflies and hundreds of other species migrate as well. Migratory species face a special challenge because they need healthy habitats in more than one location.

Everywhere, habitats are under threat. They are lost as the human population grows, which results in cities expanding into wild areas, forests being cut down and water and air polluted. These and other changes to habitats can affect the organisms living there. When a forest is logged, a bird may lose its nesting habitat. A gasoline spill can change a lake into a dangerous place for beavers, fish and birds. Turning grassland into grain fields changes a permanent habitat for dozens of plant species into a temporary home for one.

Protecting the world's biodiversity means protecting species and their habitats. This is especially true for endangered species. Habitat loss is the number one reason endangered species become extinct.

Around the world, conservation areas, parks, marine protected areas and wildlife refuges act like life rafts for Planet Ark. In these places, habitats are preserved for plants and animals. Activities such as logging and hunting are usually banned. Protected places also act like living laboratories for scientists, allowing them to observe species in the wild and learn more about what they need to survive.

On Earth, some life forms can exist in extreme habitats such as in hot vents deep on the ocean floor, where hot, sulfur-filled water bubbles up from the Earth's molten core.

The Dirt on Biodiversity

In a world that has butterflies as delicate as tissue paper and cacti with thorns as long as your finger, plain ordinary dirt may sound, well, as dull as dirt. But healthy soil is actually one of the most important links to a world alive with biodiversity.

Without healthy soil, plants can't thrive. And without plants, what would plant-eating herbivores — from emus to wombats — eat? Since plants form the base of food chains, much of Earth's biodiversity relies on what is going on in the ground below our feet. Your dinner plate would be pretty empty if Earth's soil got sick. But soil provides more than just food. Rich, diverse soil ensures that we have construction materials and fibers for clothing. It also cleans the water and air and regulates climate.

Healthy soil is a hotbed of biodiversity. In fact, soil is home to more than one-quarter of all known living species, including bacteria, fungi, algae, yeast, one-celled microbes called protozoa, ants, millipedes and tiny worms called nematodes. All of these soil dwellers recycle dead plants and animals into nutrients that plants use to grow. Then plants relay nutrients along the food chain to animals. Larger soil-dwelling animals act like engineers. Earthworms, ants, termites and even small mammals, such as moles, tunnel through the soil. Their actions create habitats for smaller organisms but also make spaces for air, water, nutrients and the roots of plants.

But around the world, soils are being damaged. Land that is farmed over and over again without time to rest and replenish becomes tired out. Crops don't do well in this overused soil. And large industrial farms grow huge fields of a single crop. This makes the crop an easy target for insects or disease. To fight them, farmers often add chemical fertilizers or pesticides, which can harm the water and soil in the long term.

Besides intensive farming, other practices, such as logging and overgrazing by cattle, can harm soils and the organisms living in them. But if we treat soil as a living thing and give it adequate food, water and even rest, it can help sustain other living things.

Good soil = good growing. And that's good for all life on Earth.

What's going on under your feet? Lots! The soil is a habitat for millions of living things, from microscopic bacteria to multi-legged millipedes. These soil dwellers help keep the soil healthy.

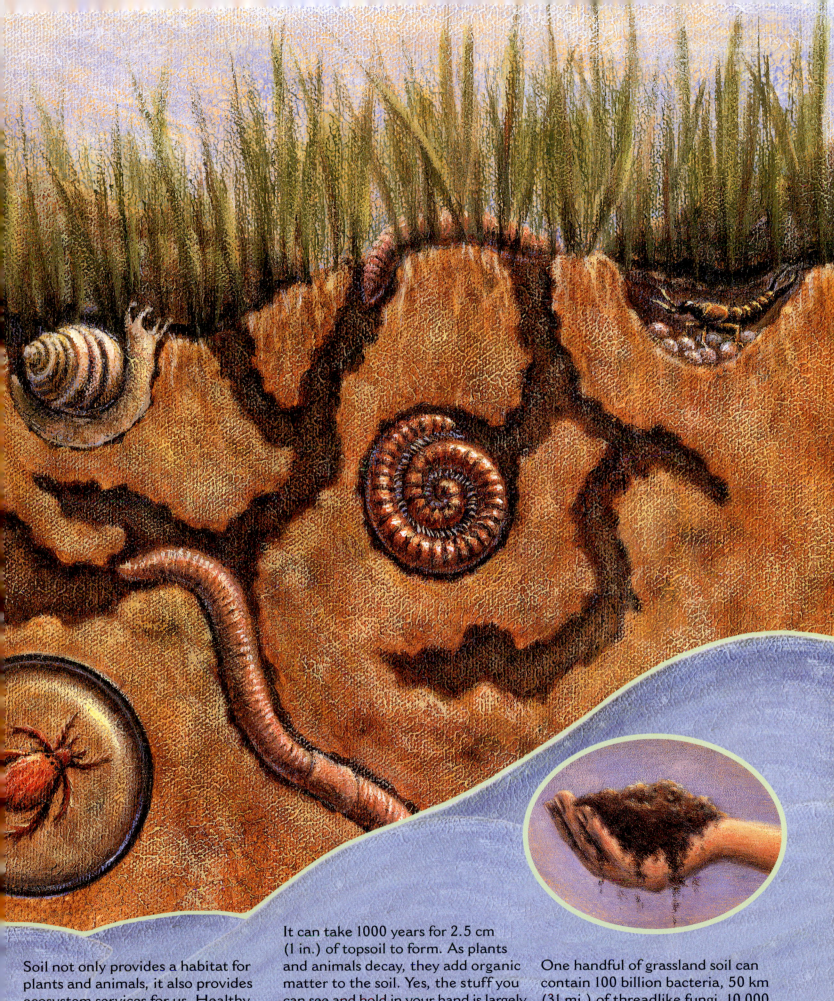

Soil not only provides a habitat for plants and animals, it also provides ecosystem services for us. Healthy soil makes for healthy plants, which can prevent erosion, keep waterways clean and even reduce the impact of global warming by taking carbon dioxide out of the air.

It can take 1000 years for 2.5 cm (1 in.) of topsoil to form. As plants and animals decay, they add organic matter to the soil. Yes, the stuff you can see and hold in your hand is largely made of dead and decomposing "bits" of once-living things, from earthworm poop to dragonfly wings and blackberry thorns. Minerals from rocks, the air and water also add nutrients to topsoil.

One handful of grassland soil can contain 100 billion bacteria, 50 km (31 mi.) of threadlike fungi, 10 000 nematode worms and 5000 insects, mites and other tiny arthropods.

The Aliens Have Landed!

No, they're not aliens from outer space. They're "alien species" right here on Earth — species that have moved or been brought into a habitat where they don't normally live. Sometimes these alien, or introduced, species weaken biodiversity by taking over habitats and pushing out native plants or animals.

Not all introduced species have a negative impact on the local species. But in some cases, the new arrival can settle in and cause a disaster. In Africa, for example, the Nile perch was introduced into Lake Victoria as a new source of fish for local people. The fish was good to eat, but it also loved *to* eat. The Nile perch began to chomp its way through the lake's native fish population. In just a few decades, it was responsible for the extinction of 200 species of fish in the lake.

A similar story began when some brown tree snakes arrived in Guam as stowaways on a cargo ship in the early 1950s. Without the snake's natural predators, its population exploded. Before too long, there were thousands of brown tree snakes. Hungry snakes. The snakes slithered their way across the island, wiping out twelve species of native birds and reducing the numbers of small lizards and mammals, including fruit bats, an important pollinator.

Introduced plant species can also take hold and become invasive, resulting in huge changes not only to native species but also to habitats. In the southern United States, for instance, the kudzu plant was introduced from Japan. Now, kudzu is called the "vine that ate the south" or the "mile-a-minute plant." It is spreading across the southern states, covering buildings and smothering native plants.

Today, countries are becoming much more aware of the problems of introduced species and taking steps to avoid them. For instance, when an aquatic plant called Eurasian milfoil threatened to spread from lake to lake in Canada, wildlife officials took action. They encouraged boaters to clean and dry their boats to kill any milfoil roots and seeds before going from one lake to the next. And on many small islands, such as Kapiti Island in New Zealand, wildlife officials are working hard to eradicate invasive intruders, such as rats that prey on birds and native mammals. They set traps for the rats and also carefully restrict the activities of people on the island. If you visit, they may even check your backpack for stowaway rats before letting you step ashore!

Brown tree snakes introduced on the island of Guam multiplied and ate their way through many native species.

Islands are often hit hard when invasive species arrive. In the Hawaiian Islands, twenty species of flightless birds became extinct because of introduced predators such as rats and mongooses.

Sometimes farm animals can act like alien species. When cattle, sheep and pigs are released into the wild, they can destroy native vegetation. And house cats are around-the-house aliens — they sometimes prey on birds, reptiles and small mammals.

In some situations, an introduced species can actually be beneficial. An introduced tree, the salt cedar, provides a valuable nesting habitat for several species of birds in the American southwest. One of the birds is the southwestern willow flycatcher, an endangered species. The alien tree is providing a habitat that may help save the bird.

Countries have signed international laws to stop the sale or trade of items such as tortoise shells, elephant tusks and tiger bones. Sadly, illegal trade has continued and still endangers some of these species.

Water can be overexploited, too. Lakes and aquifers (underground sources of water) that are drained too quickly or for too long may not have time to replenish. This can affect many species that rely on the water — including us.

Taking Too Much

Rhinoceroses are endangered because they have been hunted for their horns. Sometimes hunters shoot the animal, saw or chop off the horn and leave the body of the rhino to rot.

With a spiky horn or two on its nose, armor-like skin, tough-as-a-tank body and a reputation for being a bit cranky, the rhinoceros is one of the oddest animals on Planet Ark. It is also one of the rarest.

Today, there are five species of rhinoceros in the world, and three of them are critically endangered. As of 2012, only seven northern white rhinoceroses were thought to exist in the world. These animals are rare because of their horns. For centuries, the horns have been used to make traditional medicines. This means the animals become targets for hunters. Today, it is illegal to sell rhinoceros horns, but this makes the horns even more valuable to poachers willing to take a risk. As a result, rhinos are being threatened by overexploitation.

Overexploitation, or overharvesting, means that a species is being hunted or harvested so intensively that its survival is in danger. It is being killed faster than it can reproduce.

There are many ways that overexploitation occurs. Often it is direct — people hunt, fish or collect without considering the future.

They take too much, too quickly. This could happen to a rare medicinal plant; an animal valued for its meat, fur, antlers or tusks; or even a fish that fetches a good price. Overexploitation can also happen indirectly, when habitat is destroyed. For example, destructive logging practices can lead to soil erosion, making the area unsuitable for growing future forests.

Overexploitation is a concern around the world. To prevent it, countries often establish limits, or quotas, on how much of a resource can be harvested each year. They try to ensure that harvesting is sustainable — that enough members of a species are left to reproduce and sustain the population in the future.

Do these conservation efforts work? Sometimes. The Atlantic cod, a huge fish that can grow as long as a couch, was harvested for centuries. Then, in 1992, the cod fishery "collapsed." The fish had been overharvested. Today, after almost two decades of protection, the cod stocks seem to be slowly recovering in some areas.

In many parts of the world, predators such as wolves and cougars were once seen as "vermin." People were offered cash to shoot them on sight. Today, this attitude is changing, and predators are seen as an important part of natural systems.

The Convention for International Trade in Endangered Species (CITES) controls the trade of living things. It protects about 33 000 species.

Cooling a Warming Planet

What's the connection between coal and coral reefs, power plants and polar bears? The answer is global warming — the slow but steady heating of Earth's atmosphere. As people burn fossil fuels — coal, oil and natural gas — to power vehicles, heat buildings and manufacture everything from plastic forks to eyeglasses to car bumpers, "greenhouse gases" are released into the atmosphere. There, the gases trap the Sun's heat, driving temperatures upward. As a result, the world's climate is slowly warming.

Living things have always had to adapt to changes in their environment, but global warming is altering Earth's climate faster than some plants and animals can adjust. In the Arctic, for example, scientists are watching closely to see how polar bears adapt to changing ice cover. As ice melts, it could make it more difficult for them to hunt seals, their main prey. This means the future of polar bears is uncertain.

Sometimes global warming pushes systems out of "sync." In the oceans, for instance, the spring growth of phytoplankton — food for the larvae of many sea creatures — is happening earlier than usual. This means the food is available before many of the animals that need it have even hatched.

If you've ever stepped inside a greenhouse, you'll know that the glass traps in the heat, creating a hot climate inside that is perfect for growing plants. When fossil fuels are burned, the resulting gases act like the glass in a greenhouse. They form a layer in the atmosphere that traps the Sun's heat.

Plants take carbon dioxide — a greenhouse gas — out of the air. As the plants decay, the soil absorbs this carbon. Soil animals are also made partially of carbon. When they die, their carbon passes into the soil as well. The soil acts like a carbon sink, storing carbon underground rather than in the air, where it can contribute to global warming.

Changes in habitats may force some animals to alter their migration patterns. Some may begin their journeys earlier in the year or spread into new areas. And some will stop migrating completely. Instead, they will stay year-round in areas that were formerly too cold for a winter habitat.

Rising temperatures can disrupt weather patterns, causing droughts in some areas, floods in others. Over time, climate changes can affect habitats — and the animals that live in them. The animals may be forced to move into new habitats or face extinction. For example, in tropical areas, increasing water temperatures and changes in ocean chemistry — both caused by global warming — are killing coral reefs. As the reef habitats die, so do the animals that live in and around them.

How species adapt to climate change can vary. Some adapt quite well, while others do not, and may eventually become extinct. The loss to biodiversity of a single species may not seem all that alarming. But remember that all species are part of the same web — when one species is harmed, it can affect many others. For example, in the ocean, warming water temperatures are reducing phytoplankton, the tiny organisms that are at the base of most marine food chains. If phytoplankton populations decline too much, almost all life in the sea will be affected.

Global warming is a great concern, but there are many steps people are taking to slow and perhaps even stop it. Developing alternative energy sources (such as solar and wind power), fuel-efficient vehicles and mass-transit systems (buses, subways and trains) can reduce our use of the fossil fuels that cause global warming. Recycling Earth's precious resources, such as metals, helps, too. But one of the best things we can do is to stop buying so much stuff. The more we buy, the more we consume Earth's precious resources and contribute to global warming.

Cooling a warming planet is a big job, but it's one that has to be done to help preserve Planet Ark's rich biodiversity.

In the Arctic, global warming is melting the ice, affecting the areas where polar bears travel and hunt. These changes to their habitat are testing their ability to adapt.

When people travel together in mass-transit vehicles (buses and trains) instead of driving their own cars, less fossil fuel is burned. Even better is when the vehicles are powered by renewable energy, such as solar or wind power. The rapid-transit trains in Calgary, Alberta, run on electricity generated by wind turbines.

Many businesses offer "carbon credits" for sale when people purchase something that creates greenhouse gases, such as an air-plane flight. The money from the carbon credits is used to help reduce carbon dioxide and other greenhouse gases. It might go toward planting trees or investing in renewable energy.

Boosting Biodiversity

In 1813, John James Audubon, a painter and avid birdwatcher, was on his way to Louisville, Kentucky, when the sky turned dark. It wasn't a storm cloud — the sky was dark with birds. Flock after flock of passenger pigeons flew overhead. He made a mark in his sketchpad for every flock that passed. In twenty-one minutes, he had 163 marks. At the time, passenger pigeons were thought to be one of the world's most numerous birds, with a population of two to five million. Today, there are none. The passenger pigeon is extinct.

There are many reasons why. Passenger pigeons were easy to catch and tasted good. As forests were cleared for cities and farmland, the loss of habitat also affected the birds. In 1914, the last passenger pigeon died in the Cincinnati Zoo.

Species extinction is still happening today, but many Noahs, both individuals and organizations, are working hard to slow the loss. For instance, scientists monitor wildlife populations. If they see numbers decline, they sound a warning. Wildlife reserves and other protected areas are sometimes established to preserve precious habitats. But if a population becomes critically low, the endangered animals may become part of a captive breeding program in a zoo, wildlife preserve or other facility. The animals are bred in a clean, disease-free environment safe from predators. This gives them a good chance to survive and thrive.

If a population of captive-bred animals grows, and there is a safe place for them to live, the animals may be released back into the wild. Not long ago, the black-footed ferret was so rare that scientists thought it might be extinct. Then a small population of eighteen wild ferrets was discovered in Wyoming. They may have been the last wild black-footed ferrets anywhere in the world. After twenty-five years of captive breeding in zoos and a ferret-recovery center, the population has increased to 5800. The ferrets are slowly being reintroduced into the wild in the United States and Canada.

People are also protecting plants. Botanical gardens and other organizations save seeds, bulbs and whole plants and breed them in controlled environments to ensure that species do not become extinct.

Saving a species is important, but animals need a place to live, too, so some Noahs focus on preserving habitats. National parks often protect huge areas of wilderness, while butterfly gardens create a small area of wildlife habitat in a backyard. Big or small, every action that protects species or their habitats helps protect biodiversity on Planet Ark.

Planet Ark no longer has woolly mammoths, brontosaurs and millions of other species. Over Earth's history, living things have regularly become extinct. The difference is that today the rate of extinction is faster than ever before because of human-made changes.

Huge flocks of passenger pigeons once darkened the sky. Today they are extinct.

Almost one-third of the world's known amphibians (frogs, salamanders and their relatives) have become extinct or are threatened with extinction. Like other animals, they have been affected by loss of habitat, competition from diseases and introduced species. They are also super sensitive to pollution and climate change.

People's actions can also bring species back from the brink of extinction. For years, a pesticide called DDT was used to control insects. It also killed birds such as eagles and hawks, which fed on animals that had consumed the DDT. People raised the alarm, and DDT was banned in many parts of the world. Today, species once affected by DDT — including the bald eagle, the national bird of the United States — are recovering.

Growing Biodiversity

The next time you go to the grocery store, see how many types of carrots you can find. Chances are you will find only one — the long, slender, bright-orange variety that is Bugs Bunny's favorite. But there are actually several hundred varieties of carrots in the world, each with a slightly different shape, taste and color. Yes, not all carrots are orange — some are purple, white, yellow and even red.

The biodiversity of the food we eat is declining. Why? Mostly because of the way we farm. It used to be that farms were small and raised a variety of plants and animals. Today, most farms are larger and specialized — they grow only one crop or raise one kind of animal. It's more efficient for farmers to plant and tend one species than a variety that have different needs. The result? Less variety on your dinner plate.

Foods such as chocolate, coffee, tea and sugar are produced by poorer countries to sell to wealthier countries. To ensure that the environment is not damaged and the people growing the food are treated fairly, some groups have developed strict guidelines for products and labeled them "Fair Trade."

In India, a network of 54 seed banks and 500 000 farmers work to protect the diversity of seeds grown there. To educate people in organic farming, seed saving and food security, a learning center called Bija Vidyapeeth (School of the Seed) was established.

But it's not just a matter of variety — it's a matter of survival. Imagine having rice for every meal. This is true for almost half the world's population. Now imagine that an insect attacked the rice crop. If there was only one kind of rice, the entire crop could be wiped out, and that could lead to starvation. But, fortunately, there are thousands of varieties of rice, so the loss of one variety doesn't mean the loss of all rice. Having a diversity of rice helps keep the food supply safe.

By protecting the biodiversity of the foods we grow, we can provide food security for the world's people. Food security means that people have enough to eat and do not face hunger or starvation.

One way that modern-day Noahs have been safeguarding food crops and rare plants is through seed banks. Seed banks store seeds for the future. By locking them safely away, these banks ensure that some seeds will survive even if a plant becomes extinct in nature. Although seed banks can preserve the genetic heritage of plants, it is still better to protect plants and their habitats before they threaten to disappear forever.

In the past, farms were small and raised a variety of plants and animals. Today, there are fewer small, mixed farms. Instead, huge industrial farms raise only one crop or type of animal.

The world's largest seed is from the coco-de-mer palm tree. A single seed can weigh more than a two-year-old child and be as big as a basketball.

Rice, wheat, corn and soybeans are some of the world's most important food crops. Chances are, you've eaten several things today that contain one or more of these plants.

Why Biodiversity Matters

For billions of years, life on Earth has been evolving. The result — a rich biodiversity — is the foundation of life on our planet. And just like a strong, leak-proof hull on an ark, a healthy biodiversity supports so much.

Healthy ecosystems — Animals, plants, microbes and more make up the world's ecosystems and provide ecosystem services, from the air we breathe to the water we drink and the food we eat.

Insurance — Millions of species are yet to be discovered. We don't fully understand all of the ways in which species are interconnected. By protecting biodiversity, we ensure options for the future.

Human health — A healthy environment keeps humans healthy, too. Polluted and damaged habitats often contribute to poverty and illness. Also, many of the medicines we use come from natural plant sources.

Employment — A rich biodiversity can provide jobs. We harvest resources such as fish and timber, grow crops in the soil and travel the world to experience different habitats and cultures.

Human rights — When biodiversity is protected and ecosystems are intact and healthy, the world's people have a better chance of getting enough food, shelter, clean air and water and even employment.

Inspiration — Artists, writers, dancers, musicians and even scientists gain inspiration from the natural world. Most people, in fact, find that spending time in natural areas — whether they are hiking, fishing, gardening or just sitting on a shoreline gazing at the view — adds to their happiness and health.

Just because — While there are many reasons to preserve biodiversity, we don't really need a reason. This isn't just a planet for people. It's a planet — and an ark — for all living things.

Everyone can do something to help the world's biodiversity. Your idea can be simple and small, or you can dream big, as Felix Finkbeiner did. When he was nine, Felix learned about global warming and wanted to do something. His idea? To plant a million trees in every country on Earth! He started a group called Plant for the Planet in his home country of Germany. Their motto is "Stop Talking. Start Planting." Felix and other children of Plant for the Planet are modern-day Noahs. To read about other Noahs, turn the page, and then read on to see how you can become a Noah, too. We all can make a difference.

Scientists have been inspired by everything from spiderwebs to bat echolocation to create materials and technologies that we use today. This is called biomimicry.

The government of Bhutan uses a "happiness index" to measure the well-being of its people. This index takes into account the health of the natural environment.

Spending time in green spaces is good for your health. Studies show that parks and natural areas not only provide places for recreation but also give people a sense of relaxation and general well-being.

Modern-Day Noahs

Around the world, groups and individuals of all ages are taking steps large and small to help protect biodiversity. Like Noah, they want to help preserve the world's species and the habitats they need.

Volunteers from Tree New Mexico **planted 3000 trees** along the Rio Salado. The trees anchor the soil and prevent erosion. Now, the once murky river runs clear. Trees not only help save the soil — a single broad-leaved tree that lives for 100 years can absorb 1 ton of carbon dioxide, a greenhouse gas that contributes to global warming.

Did you know that acting can be good for the environment? Fifteen-year-old Muthamizh from India **started a street theater group** to educate people about global warming and climate change. More than 4000 people have watched her theater troupe's shows, and she has inspired fourteen other youth groups to form environmental clubs.

Students at Nashville's Lockeland Design Center Elementary School are **composting their waste** from school lunches. Instead of becoming garbage, the orange peels, bread crusts and other lunch leftovers are composted into nutrient-rich soil. Other schools keep **worms in their classrooms** to help make compost. The worms gnaw through food scraps, creating rich soil for school gardens.

Along the Pacific Flyway — a bird migration route between South America and the Arctic — students participating in the Shorebird Sister Schools Network **monitor birds** when they make a "pit stop" in their community. They count the birds and let other schools along the route know they are on the way. These students are volunteer "citizen scientists." Their work helps scientists monitor shorebird populations and note any changes in their migration patterns over time.

Pollination Guelph is **creating a habitat for pollinators** in their Ontario town. This includes a Pollination Park on the site of an old garbage dump. You can create your own pollination park at home. Any plant that has a flower will attract insects and perhaps even hummingbirds.

Sean, a teenager from Florida, **helps marine life** with his Stow It, Don't Throw It project. His group makes containers that give fishermen a place to put their used fishing line. That keeps the nylon line out of the ocean so that fish and sea mammals don't get entangled.

When she was six years old, Sarah from New York State started a lemonade and hot chocolate stand to **raise money** for projects that help people and the planet. She also started a website, Project LemonAid, which provides young people with ideas for their own money-raising projects. Her motto? "Saving the Earth, one cup at a time"!

Students at Upper Cape Cod Regional Technical School **installed a wind turbine** to produce energy for their school. The students not only learned important skills that will help them in the future, but also helped offset the school's electricity bills.

The summer after she finished elementary school, Adeline became concerned by the loss of mangroves in her country, Indonesia. Mangroves help protect shorelines. When they are missing, the damage from hurricanes and tsunamis is more devastating. Adeline **formed a club** called Sahabat Alam, which means "friends of nature," to encourage students to help the environment. Students have tackled projects such as planting mangroves, cleaning beaches and protecting turtle-breeding habitats.

Taylor and Peyton from Merrickville, Ontario, collected 450 kg (1000 lb.) of hair from salons and their friends and family to send to the Gulf of Mexico, where it was used to **soak up oil** after a massive oil spill.

When Max was in grade seven, he learned how to build a solar oven at his Ohio school. That year, he also learned that some people in Uganda had to walk for hours just to gather enough wood for cooking. He found out more about solar ovens and eventually traveled to Uganda, where he helped villagers **build solar ovens**. Using these ovens, the villagers can cook without cutting trees for firewood.

In Chicago, volunteers **help birds that have collided with windows** in downtown buildings, where lights confuse the birds. They also lobbied for "dark skies" in the city. As a result, Chicago is the first city in the United States to go dark after 11 p.m. during the spring and fall migrations.

Eric **started a plant patrol** near his home in Utah to remove the invasive plant dalmatian toadflax. The plant has changed the habitat of many native plants and animals. Eric knew that the job was a big one, so he talked to youth groups, such as 4-H clubs and Girl Scouts, to teach them how they can safely remove toadflax and other invasive plants. His efforts have helped to renew local habitats for insects, songbirds and mammals.

*Students from Jean Vanier Intermediate Catholic School and St-Laurent Academy in Ottawa, Ontario, are **protecting and studying a natural wetland** as part of their Macoun Marsh Biodiversity Project. They have identified more than 1307 species of plants and animals in the wetland.*

You Can Be a Noah, Too

Can just one kid make a difference to biodiversity? You bet. Anything you can do to conserve Planet Ark's precious resources and keep the land, water and air clean helps biodiversity. Here are a few ideas to get you going.

Practice the three Rs: Reduce, Reuse and Recycle. Then add three more: Rethink — do you really need it? Refuse — say "no, thanks" to plastic shopping bags and single-use disposable products, such as cups and pens. Rejoice — get outside to explore and enjoy the natural world around you!

Conserve water. Turn off the tap while you brush your teeth. Use an ice cube to cool your drink rather than running the water to cool it. Take a shower (a short one) rather than a bath. The less water we use, the less needs to be gathered, cleaned and delivered to your home. All these actions save energy.

Conserve energy. Turn off the lights when you leave a room. Put on a sweater rather than turning up the heat. Use the dishwasher or washing machine only when there is a full load. Electricity is generated in many ways, such as damming rivers, harnessing solar power and using nuclear reactors. When we conserve energy, we minimize the need for more of these projects. And saving energy also reduces the level of greenhouse gases released to our environment.

Save resources. Use both sides of a piece of paper. Think before you use a computer printer — do you really need to print it out? Buy products with less packaging and minimize your use of plastics. When you consume less, it takes pressure off our planet's precious resources.

Plant a garden in your yard or on your deck or windowsill. Grow foods you can eat and reduce the greenhouse gases otherwise used to transport foods. Or grow native plants and trees that local wildlife will enjoy.

Ride your bike, skateboard or scooter, or take the bus instead of asking your parents to drive you everywhere. It's good for you and for the environment.

Be a citizen scientist. There are dozens of projects that you can participate in to help scientists learn about wildlife or nature. Look for Frog Watch, Project Feeder Watch, Ice Watch, Plant Watch and even Worm Watch!

Never release unwanted pets, such as goldfish, rabbits or cats, into the wild. Find an adoptive home instead. Releasing a pet is not fair to the animal. It was once cared for, but now it needs to fend for itself. As well, a domestic pet can become an invasive species that has an impact on native plants and animals.

Learn what species or spaces are at risk in your area and then find out what you can do to help.

Be a soil saver. Plant trees on slopes or cleared areas to prevent the soil from eroding, and do whatever you can to improve the soil. This includes adding compost and not using toxic pesticides.

Speak up! Share your ideas and what you have learned about biodiversity with your friends. Every ship — even Planet Ark — needs an able crew to keep it sailing and safe!

Glossary

biodiversity: the variety of life on Earth

climate change: the change in weather (temperature, wind patterns and precipitation) over time

ecosystem: all of the organisms that live in an environment, as well as the nonliving things (such as climate) that affect living things

ecosystem services: the services that organisms provide for the planet, such as oxygen production

endangered: a species that is in danger of becoming extinct

erosion: the washing or wearing away of soil by water or wind

extinct: a species that no longer exists anywhere on Earth

food chain: a way of describing how food energy passes from one organism to another (for example, a mouse eats seeds and an owl eats a mouse)

fossil fuels: coal, oil and natural gas, which can be used to create energy

genetic diversity: the diversity within one species. For example, humans are all the same species, but genetic diversity makes each of us different.

global warming: the gradual warming of the Earth's atmosphere that can lead to climate change

habitat diversity: the variety of natural places (habitats) where organisms live

habitats: the natural places where species find water, food and shelter

introduced species: species that move or have been moved into a habitat where they don't normally live

migration: the movement of animals between two or more habitats during the year

overexploitation: when so much of a species is harvested, hunted or caught that its survival is in danger

pollination: the spreading of pollen from one plant to another by insects, animals or the wind

species: a group of organisms that breed with one another and produce offspring

species diversity: the variety of different species on Earth

Index